LEOPARDS, HARES, DRAGONS AND BEARS!
"THE ADVENTURES OF TOMMY TEWLIGAN"

by

Christopher Ronay

Illustrations by Stefanie St. Denis

Leopards, Hares, Dragons and Bears! "The Adventures of Tommy Tewligan"

ILLUSTRATIONS: Stefanie St. Denis
LAYOUT: Debbi Stocco

ISBN 13: 978-0-9863507-6-4

Printed in the USA

To Mom for showing me the ways of the Leopards, Hares, Dragons and Bears.

Chapter I

"To some a song of soothing lull, to me a stomping angry troll."

Once when I was a child,
        about the age you are right now,
                a magical summer came to be
                        from which I'll tell you how.

I lived within a smallish house that rested halfway down,
along a quiet street you see, within a quiet town.
And in this house were only two; my mother and myself;
a cozy house a lot like yours with dust upon the shelf.

Now this may seem quite nice to you,
but one thing kept ringing loud and true.
However hard I tried and tried,
my fear was one I couldn't hide.

So bad my fear that even though an early rooster starts his crow,
just that to welcome in the day…

To me a **MONSTER** comes this way!

And even though the thunders wrath alerts the earth of coming bath;
to some a song of soothing lull…

To me a stomping angry **TROLL**!

A fearful kid as you can tell,
        my life that timid trend;
                so scared I was of everything…
                        But that was soon to end!

One morning came as they had before; those same soft steps on the worn wooden floor, from quiet clop of hurried shoe and my Mother's voice; at that instant I knew.

"Wake up wake up you sleepy little shrew! To work I go and for you… go too!"

"What a night, what a dream," as I bound where I lay, "I thought that I dreamt that together we'd play!"

"To play maybe yours", she grinned, "as for me I must toil. The nursing home calls and the bedpans my foil. Well deserved it may be…It's your summer bed, but with Grandma away, Porter Stone Manor…instead.

So give me this promise and to you I give mine; no trouble you cause- No deed out of line, then the night will be ours however YOU make, with lots of balloons or a sparkling bright cake."

6

"Can I jump off the bed and air run in my socks?

Shoot rubber bands at the cat and build forts out of blocks?"

"It can be however you want", she replied, "It's yours to create;
So put on your shoes and that sock with its mate,

TICK TOCK
TICK TOCK
THERE'S NO TIME TO DEBATE
NOW SCURRY AND HURRY FOR IN MINUTES
WE'RE LATE!"

As we ran to the car, my legs slowing a trace, from thoughts of this day in that HORRIBLE place. The head nurse at the home with her terrible sneer and Porter Stone Manor like a dungeon of fear.

Mom started the car to a

Bang and a Glug,

a Sputter a Spurt

and one THUNDEROUS tug!

In no time at all we'd finished the race, when out popped a frown behind

MUSTACHE and face.

I called him a frown; he was really a guard, who stood rather squatty and grimaced quite hard. He guarded a gate to the entrance at work and circled the car with a scowl and a smirk.

The frown began tapping his pen to his chin,
Tapping and tapping
Till two turned to ten.
He glared and he mumbled deciding our fate,
Then spinning his pen shrieked…

"OPEN THE GATE!!"

The road wound ahead and narrowed from sight. First it went left and then it went right. Giant trees in a row like soldiers in file, LOOMED down from above and stretched for a mile. Up through the car window and piercing a cloud rose Porter Stone Manor in shadow draped shroud.

And just when I began SH SHIVERING with fear, a jingle of keys and Mom's voice cried… "WE'RE HERE."

"Why must you work?" I pleaded. "I don't want us to stay.
Let's run from this place; let's not work on this day!"

"OH NO", she said. "NO! This can't possibly be! A promise is a promise once you promise you see. And as promises go, your promise to me, was the strongest a promise as promises be!"

Well this wasn't the first and would not be the last. She'd made some decisions… which worked well in the past; and I'd given my promise, for that she was right, but my fear… It still lingered and held with its might.

I unlocked the car door, a slight wind hit my hair. High atop of the manor, Gargoyles panted out air. Their stony cold grimace gave my throat quite a lump, with pitiless eyes peering down from their stump.

> I squeezed her hand tight from Gargoyles galore,
> As we walked up the stairs to an opening door…

❖❖❖

A long hallway of blurry,

This maze was a scurry

Of snipping swift legs

Like scissors in hurry!

Behind her I stuck

As we conquered this muck;

When nurse station was made.

Still behind her I stayed!

I slowly peeked my head out as we stopped on a dime and saw all the nurses standing straight in a line. Underneath a large chair tapped shoes with a rattle and two hulking legs with hose losing the battle.

The head nurse as they called her face red as a fire; her eyes darkly cold and as thin as a *wire*. On her cheek was a mole that had hair like a spider and two globby doughnuts oozed closely beside her.

Her shoes ticked like a bomb…then she pointed towards mom.

"TWO times you've been tardy", BOOMED her voice rather hardy!
"ONE more and you go on my list.
Chop chop, don't delay or I'm docking your pay.
This instant in line… I INSIST!"

She then backed from her chair. A dreadful screech filling the air. You know the sound that it makes; like a train slamming on brakes. Not an eye met her doom as she circled the room- quickly gazing on me, as I shrunk to a pea!

"As for you little worm", her huff puffing my hair; "I'll give you this warning, so take care and beware! Cross my ears, or my nose, or my stare if you dare, and you'll hang by your feet beside those that you care!

I'm going to say this once and once for you all,
Life's not meant to be fun…It's not meant for a ball;
So laughing and clapping are NOT sounds that you make;
Joking and poking would be one awful mistake!
My laws you must heed and must heed for your sake!" And then there was hush as she crammed in a cake.

"PSST!" Came a call, then a
WHISTLE and a
CLICK.

"A task I must ask, so come here and quite quick!"

Waving to me from his chair;

In manner astute…Sat a crumpled old man in green hat and grey suit.

"I have a matter you see- something quite crucial!"

My mother simply smiled and nodded her approval.

❖❖❖

Chapter II

"A journey you must take in a land quite strange from here."

I noticed that his hands were clasping rather tight;

Streaming through his fingers shined bright and glowing light. He opened up his grasp, pouring forth a golden flame;

Two tiny *wings* unfolded
Two spiny *tails* the same.
The *head* was that of DRAGON
The *body* that of BEAR
The *legs* were that of LEOPARD
The tiny *feet* of HARE.

My eyes on the Creature and the Creature alone as the old man spoke in slow textured tone.

"This Being in my hands is being bound with you. His future holds uncertain; his subjects lie askew. And being that this Being is a Being bound with you, his kingdom YOU must unite…his throne YOU must renew!"

I can't believe my eyes, I thought.

       This can't be what I think.

A strangely Creature moves before;

       My eyes they cannot blink.

"I know not who you are." I said. "Where is this land you've told?

       What is this that you ask of me?

       I'm only eight years old!"

"I'm a friend." he said. "So have no fear." He told me with a wink.
"This land you see is far from here, but closer than you think. I only ask you follow close your heart and inner core. So trust me when I tell you that, I ask for nothing more.

A journey you must take in a land quite strange from here. Many friends you will to make…and many foes you will to fear! This task I must entrust you; alone our secret keep. Your kindness to employ, then courage alone you reap. This voyage I would take, if my years much nearer you; I can show the one true way…

But it's YOU who must jump through!"

This old man had a peaceful face that I could peer right through, and in his voice I felt a trust of someone that I knew. I can't believe what came out next, it didn't seem like me that nodded yes to this request of that most shockingly.

Just then I felt a tiny scratch upon my fingers bare.

Within my hands the Creature stood.

Within my hands we paired!

"You see!" The old man whispered. "You're already halfway there! Now put him in your pocket; our secret safe from view, and follow right behind me- I'll show the way for you."

We came upon a dim lit room all filled with coats and dust…

"Many choices here to make", he said, "your inner voice to trust. This room begins your journey on; and not just one of any. There are countless worlds within this room…Choose wise among the many!"

Some coats were long and lanky,

Some fat with lots of fluff.

Some coats were rather flashy

And some that felt quite rough.

Some coats were softly silky and smallish in their shape;

What came to me most strikingly…was hooded purple cape!

The old man beamed a pleasing grin and spoke with soothing voice.

"I see you made a brilliant pick; you made a perfect choice. Within this world the choice is yours to act in which you may, but may you act most recklessly then reckless his world will stay. Your cape will take you to his land, so hide to quickly find; some place in which

17

you can recall and keep well within your mind. Conceal the cape without delay, upon this vital track. And know that when I tell you it...Will also bring you back!"

I put the cape upon my arms
The hood upon my head.
My ears were opened widely,
My eyes I closed instead.

Silence began to fade away.   The wind began to blow.

The room began to spin around. My cape began to GLOW!!!

First it felt like falling, but then I thought I flew, right through three giant circles of...

Yellow,

Red

and Blue.

And then it felt like sliding down a damp and hollow tree.

YEP, I'm surely sliding down…and sliding swift and free!

I landed with a sudden THUD!

Right straight onto some soggy mud.

I tapped twice on the tree as there was nothing I could see.

SHHHHHH!

I hear a muddle of voices!!!

❖ ❖ ❖

Chapter III

EVIL SOON AFOOT CHEER

"PEEN GO HAAAAA   ING GO HAAAAA   GEEN GO HAAAA

WEEEEEEEEEEE!!!!

PEEN GO HAAAAA   ING GO HAAAAA   GEEN GO HAAAA

BEEEEEEEEEE!!!!

I pulled back the hood from atop of my head to hear a bit better what the voices had said. As my eyes soon adjusted its dizzy dark sight,
a tree archway before, came clear to my right…

And through it the sun shining warm golden light.

Slowly peeking my head out this archway with heed,
For I really and truly don't want noticed indeed!
And what did I see most astonishingly?
A procession of PIGS prancing loud and with glee.

But not ordinary pigs from what I could tell; well apart from their ears and their snout and their smell. Each of them carrying a large tray and quite fat- Each of them wearing a white fluffy chef's hat.

Remembering to remove my cape; for with it was a sure ESCAPE!
To keep it hidden far from view, these words were ringing loud and true.

"I believe that inside this tree should well do!!!"

But my nose started tingling…at that moment I knew…what escaped was not me but a giant…

"ACHOOOOOOOO!!!!!"

The voices stopped chanting…
I backed in the tree.
Footsteps came closer. "Why their coming for ME!!!"

I tried and I tried to recover my cape when sunlight was broken by looming pig shape. The tree wasn't giving an inch to my shoving, as I backed further in from the pig that was coming! Till into this tree he was soon with me; as he grunted and snorted inquisitively.

"M-M-My name is Tommy Tewligan", I said. Extending a quivering hand.

"I arrived from inside this tree you see; I come from a faraway land."

He fixed his eyes right on me; helpless I was to flee, for just then he coldly pointed and squealed a high pitched…

"HEEEEEEEEE!"

Before I knew he picked me up and out that hollow tree and tossed me atop a giant tray, despite my deepest plea! Their marching resumed, as I bounced high on the tray; as to where we were going was wherever they say.

The road began to spiral around a steep and rocky ridge. Then up and down and over they marched across a stony bridge. Through the mist a castle arose and trumpets began to roar; then metal clanked from straining chains which raised a wooden door.

A thousand people lined a hall of shiny glittered marble and stomped their feet in unison while hailing our arrival. At hallways end a giant throne, all draped in velvet plush; a rapping cane and rising Queen…invoked an *eerie* hush.

The pig leaned down to glaring queen and whispered in her ear, then placed my tray upon the floor which brought a wicked sneer.

"Behold our honored guest!" She said, lifting her bony hand and tapped my nose most forcefully… "He comes from strangers' land!

SO WHAT SHALL WE DO WITH THIS UGLY LITTLE TROLL?
SHALL WE ROLL HIM IN FLOUR TO COOK IN A BOWL?
SHALL WE STUFF HIM WITH APPLES TO ROAST IN A PIT?
OR GLAZE HIM WITH SUGAR AND TWIRL ON A SPIT?"

She then snapped her finger with loud splitting whip.

I felt a twinge of prickly pain, from biting on my lip. Two subjects met before us and unrolled a giant scroll; appearing were large letters as dark as blackened coal.

"I have another fate for him!" Her cold hand cupped my chin. "WE'LL HAVE HIM READ THE WORDS!" She hissed with wide and wicked grin.

"These words you are about to read have been with us for ages.
Where they come from no one knows, but obey you must the pages."

I shook my head with certain dread; my voice began to wobble.
Confused I was from what I read, as this is what it said…

> A CHILD COMES FROM STRANGERS' LAND,
> AND SO A NATION'S VOICE.
> HE TAKES FROM TRIBES THEIR HIGHEST PRIZE,
> A RULER FROM HIS CHOICE.

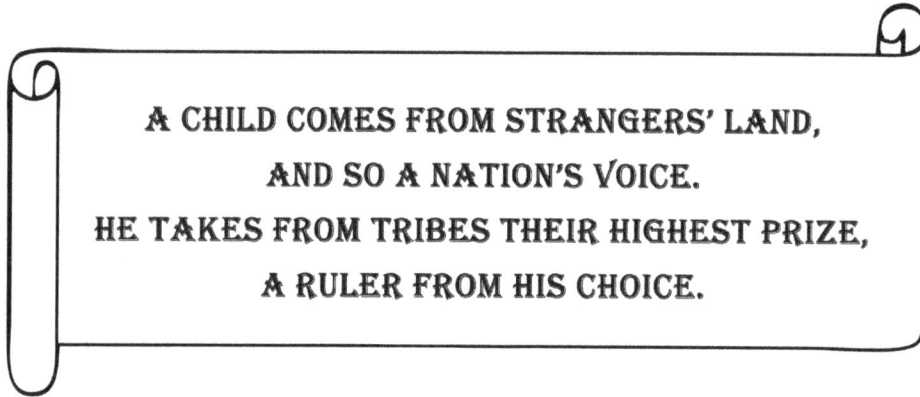

"LOOK at this!" The queen said. "He can read, we can see! Now you listen closely and only listen to me! You see it is written worm…your pathway lies ahead. To the tribes you enter trusting; a THIEF you'll leave instead!

The LEOPARDS have a **SPEARHEAD** of crystal glowing light;
The HARES, they hold a **BOOKLET** kept deep and far from sight.
DRAGONS play a magic **LYRE** that keeps a golden tune;
BEARS, they guard a weathered stone…an ancient written **RUNE**.

And so you go to each of them,

And tell them little lies,

Returning rightly back to me

With stolen precious prize.

Then voice the words of prophecy;

My evil kingdom rise.

AND WITH YOUR CHOICE YOU WILL TO MAKE ME QUEEN TO NATION'S EYES!"

"This can't be right!" I said rather slight. And so my eyes I covered.
Footsteps spoke of circling Queen, above me slowly hovered.

"I command you!" she said, her nose to mine. "Or face my fury wrath!

I'll send you to the putrid pit to take a SPIDER bath!"

All eyes to me as I glanced around…a warming face could not be found.

Came a scratching in my pocket?

My body quickly froze;

But not the tiny Creature's.

He jumped up and bit her on the nose!

"YOWWWW!!!" The Queen screeched with a terrible scowl. Then quick as a whip with Cobra-like ZIP, holding high to unveil; she'd swiped him by the tail.

"LET HIM GO!" I reached up from below.

"This Creature is my friend. This Creature I know."

The Queen snickered with glee dangling Creature to me.

"OH how adorable…now isn't that touching. You care so much for this Creature I'm clutching. Now listen to me you cantankerous flea!

You will do as I say or the CAGE he will STAY! So quick to your wits and be light on your feet; my throne you bestow…my fate not to cheat. Until you return from these tasks you complete, this Creature will live in a cage as my treat!"

The crowd began stomping as I walked towards the door,

stomping

and stomping- till they rattled the floor.

As I turned back to look towards the Creature through tear. Above the Queen's throne were these words awfully clear.

The pigs followed me out and pointed the way; one gave me a shove to my further dismay. They snorted with order like a sergeant in drill; another quick shove sent me

tumbling

down

hill.

I tumbled and tumbled…rolling down the steep pass.
My world was a blur of sky blue and green grass!

Till the steepness was welcomed with rolling soft ground and a clear shallow stream
with white water abound! Oh this water was crisp and felt good at this place, as I dipped my
hands in splashing fresh on my face. And in gulps I did drink which soon ended my thirst;
oh this water was different, such a positive burst!

I scurried down valleys of dark spongy green, and hopped nimbly over that clear
shallow stream. I followed the stream till its end…what a view!

Below me a waterfall…I leapt in with…

"WOOO HOOO!"

I then swam to the edge and crawled up on the shore,

Coughed out some cold water-then coughed out a bit more.

I laid on the ground the sun kneading my back, when two spotted legs came of **ORANGE** and **BLACK**!

❖❖❖

Chapter IV

The Soar of Lone Voice!

I slowly looked up, shielding sun from my sight as a Leopard looked down with toothy wide bite. "This spear in your side bids you well to abide! To intrude on our land brings the judgment of sand- Now rise to your feet so our eyes they can meet!"

I'm up with a JUMP as he instructed in haste and noticed I stood barely up to his waist. The tall Leopard leaned down and gave me a sniff, making the hairs on my neck stand up rather stiff.

"Why you're just a child unaided and mild. What reason you have here alone in my wild?"

My mind began searching for what I could say,
Should I bid the Queen's wishes and lie as I may?
Or make up a story all grand and aloof?

And just as I spoke what came out was…the TRUTH! I told him the story of home far away. I told him of flying and falling today. I told him of bouncing high up on a tray. I even explained what Queen's orders did say!

"As you spoke of your story I saw clear in your eyes that the story you spoke of was not spoken with lies. But clever is this Queen and she not quickly denied; so you will stand in the sand till true nature is tried."

Walking out of the trees and appearing in stride came a gang of tall Leopards tightly grouped in a pride. One motioned me forth with a flick of a claw; soon engulfed in their woods I walked with them all.

They were polite and quite nice, but still marched with a pace; and surrounded by pride seemed to be my right place. When way deep in the woods came a call from the hordes spoke from spirited banter of young Leopards with swords.

We parted these Leopards and straight through a wide path; the Leopards they stared… I saw a poke and a laugh. We came to a ridge, our way sliced through a pass, when down Leopards cheered from their hillsides of grass.

The Leopard pride stopped with a crossing of spears that pointed the way through a muddle of jeers. At the edge of a dune stood the King Leopard in gold…

"Look down", he now said, "to events that unfold!"

A young warrior was growling and stomping the sand;

A crashing of waves battered up where he stand.

A trial it seemed without judge or a jury as sand slowly moved and spelled out the word…

FURY

One section behind me let out a loud roar as the eager young warrior ran off down the shore. The King Leopard in gold slowly nodded to me- the cheering grew fainter as I crept to the sea.

I stood in the sand…my legs starting to shake,
when came a slow movement from up under the wake!

The words began forming for all who could see. In concert the crowd loudly roared…

LOYALTY

The stomping of spears pulsed my beat from the shore, when a voice from the crowd yelled… "The sand, it writes more!"

A CHILD'S EYES TO SEE THE WAY;
A CHILD'S EARS TO KNOW.
A CHILD'S MIND TO READ THE WORDS;
A CHILD'S TEARS TO GROW.

The King Leopard in gold raised his arms in a rush, which sent all the grumbling to a ghostly cold hush.

"This boy came to us armed with truth and a task. And as he is Loyal, all he need is to ask. As Leopards we hold Loyalty highest of all; and Loyalty was written, as we all can recall.

We can help with this journey…a journey quite kind; a trait that would do well for us ALL to remind. He is bound with another imprisoned by Queen. Our crystal will shine when course cannot be seen."

The crystal spearhead was heavy and covered my hand; I thanked the King Leopard for his honor and stand. He tilted his head and with a tip of his spear, pointed to a path winding left of my ear. Through the dunes it would wind and up rather high; I stopped for a moment to wave my goodbye. As the dunes became hills I looked down to rejoice, for on the shoreline was written…

THE SOAR OF LONE VOICE!

❖ ❖ ❖

Chapter V

"Originality we see; a most valued trait we all agree!"

 I hopped over soft mounds

and ducked through the thick brush,

meandered around boulders

till my face was red flush.

I turned through a corner when I heard a pierced shrill!

And saw a large flock of birds flying over a hill. The birds started turning and flying towards me! Straight at me they flew in the shape of a **V.** They reached me in seconds with a deafening screech and hovered and pecked me one and one after each!!

There was no place to hide, as I swatted and swung,

I flailed,

I fluttered,

I fortuitously flung,

And landed a blow with a monstrous smash! What was dazed was no bird, but a flying MUSTACHE! A mousy high pitch came from down under my knees.

"This way if you will, follow me if you please!" A furry white paw motioned up through the thicket, "This way if you will, follow me…I'm a WICKETT!"

I jumped through the tangles, slid down a rock face; the Mustaches shrieked but in time did not chase! The Wickett was smallish resembling a hare and dashed through the brush as if gliding on air. I tried and I tried to chase the Wickett in haste; but to follow this hare meant many breaths I would waste…and why would he run at a pace I can't top? Frustrated and angry I screamed loudly… "NOW STOP!"

I found myself fuming and thinking ill thought, as I sat on the ground wringing my hands in a knot. I kicked up clouds of dry dirt and spoke with a spit- I even began calling that fluffy Wickett a twit!

The hare crept up lightly and scratching his chin. "Forgive me my swiftness." He said with a grin. "So what manner are you?" He asked rather coy. I told him my name and that I was only a boy.

"A boy I've not heard of; I'm puzzled indeed. Your story to tell of, I'm slightly intrigued. But first we must get you to our most sacred of grounds. As I'm afraid you've encountered a flock of the *FROWNS!*"

We ambled through fissures and rambled through cracks, sauntered and shimmied through the knick and the knacks. Till walls of the cavern looked like crashing gray waves and wind began whistling through the openings in caves. We entered a cave, the wind slowed to a moan, when darkness gave way to cathedral of stone. From deep in the cave many rooms flickered with light; the splattering shadows of stirring hares in delight!

As we walked past the rooms, peering in for a glance, I saw six tiny Wicketts leaping high in a dance. Some of the hares rehearsed plays in their room, while others were singing superbly in tune.

The Wickett soon came to a large wooden door…
He thumped it three times and stomped twice on the floor.
The door opened up with a nasally snore.
At a table sat Wicketts…a council of four.

My Frowns started fading as I inched into sight, as up on the stage was a hare centered in light. And what he was doing that held all eyes in the room…was juggling three shoes and a dusty old broom!

The council of four slowly turned to discuss. They whispered and murmured and raised such a fuss. Then one of them pointed to a shelf in a crook; I heard her faint whisper…

"Look now at the book!"

A book on the shelf began painting a scene. It showed the young hare being teased rather mean. Then painted him wearing a mask amongst others. Lastly it showed him standing on the heads of his brothers. The book went blank till the end of the show; then emerged on the page was the word…

EGO

The council was silent…the book closed with a *THWAP!* And the hare left the room without even a clap. Before I knew it, I was lead up on the stage; when the book opened up to all eyes on its page.

The Wickett spoke first; began addressing the few; said I was a boy and that was all that he knew. The council began shifting in their seats from my view when one of them stood and said… "Well, what can you do?"

I pondered and thought, for several minutes too long.
I thought I might whistle my most favorite song.
I tried really hard to recall poems I'd read; when then it just hit me…
I can stand on my head!

The book began painting as I stood on my head;

elaborately painted me sleeping soundly in bed.

Then the creature was shown in his cage where he lie.

And then I was laughing…flying high in the sky!

As I stood back up straight- a little dizzy to see, four furry white faces nodding at the word…

ORIGINALITY

The council was clapping as I jumped off the stage, but gasping ensued as the book turned its page.

SO TRUST YOU MUST THE LOWER PATH,
TO SEE THE LIGHTS AHEAD,
AND FEEL THE CRY OF HOWLING WIND,
THE HIGHER PATH INSTEAD.

One Wickett stood and began her speak through gestured paws and winded squeak.

"This thing called boy as the book did tell, showed forth his life; a life lived well. And for these words, as the book did show, what they mean…only HE may know."

High up I stood above the stares…my turn to speak amongst the hares.

I told them that, what they had seen was Creature held by evil's Queen.

My pathway set to help unfold, a peaceful life that's yet untold.

And with this book I asked them part, through heavy hand and tugging heart.

As through this act true peace will pave; a Creature's life this book will SAVE!

As you might guess this caused a stir of fretted words and frenzied fur. An elder stood to voice a plea; eight nodding ears did soon agree.

"This book has been for countless years,

our source of joy and many tears.

And now it wrote one word to see.

The word it wrote was…

ORIGINALITY.

Originality we see; a most valued trait we all agree.
To release this book may be a hasty call,
but then wouldn't it also be, most…Original?"

And so it came upon this day, the Wickett joy for peace gave way. Their possessions held no fortunes take if one life was lost for possession's sake.

The book they handed freely; even put it in a sack, that fit me rather nicely and tied around my back. I thanked the tiny Wicketts for their charity and their trust. But when I turned around to go, I felt my knapsack thrust!

The booklet jumped into my hands;

I opened up to peer.

The pages turned, the words appeared…

CHOOSE TO LIVE NO FEAR!

Once again it puzzled me to see these words appear.

Just how could someone choose to live a life without a fear?

The Wickett council smiled at me and with a fluffy wave, guided me to lighted path outside their jagged cave. The walkway lit, went down a way, until a wooded brush; and soon the night then covered me in chilling silent hush.

My only sight was star-streaked light.

My only thought was strife.

And still I plunged into the night,

to taste unsheltered life.

❖❖❖

Chapter VI

Soon I Teacher of Love

Arush of wind soon hit my back; a swift and breezy push. Then up above a ghastly crack; in front a sudden *WHOOOSH*! I quickly lay upon the ground to decipher more this wind and sound. But nothing came from this debate-

And so I chose to end my wait!

As I slowly stood and dusted off, a lonely leaf went flying soft. Straight to the trees it caught the winds; a strident *CRACK* above descends! The trees, they closed so fast and true; a whoosh of wind did soon ensue. I then found out with much chagrin, the crack above would soon begin a mighty tree and trunk quite wide to quickly SNIP from side to side!

Within the trees a stick I threw- they quickly snipped that stick in TWO!

Another crack…another whoosh;

    my eyes averse to see,

        a downhill path a MILE wide

            of those horrid snipping trees!

I thought to run back up the hill, right to the Hares in tranquil still. This tranquil still held much appeal, for memories to hoard, but tranquil still meant staying still…and I was moving forward!

I noticed that the trees would crack before the rapid slice and counted that with timely steps, I could progress quite nice. The key to moving onward through this overwhelming task, was taking two steps forward, but only ONE step back. And so began my journey on, the hardest part the step that starts the journey forward but leaves behind regret.

Two steps forward.
One step back.
A whoosh of wind behind and front;
another mighty *CRACK*!

Two steps forward.
One step back,
and kept a careful eye,
until I reached the final whoosh and breathed a thankful sigh.

In the distance lights appeared…I heard a ghostly song; a wailing floating on the wind, of many voices strong. At first I flinched and tightened up and fear began to creep, but then I came to feel this song and love began to seep. I felt this song and followed forth as chorus did implore; soon surrounded me a choir of a THOUSAND wolves…or more! And then I heard the most striking song- it echoed in my core. Down below a moonlit lake and Dragons played the score!

The joyous howls soon fevered pitch; contained I could no more! And HOWL I did and ran with wolves, to the edges of the shore! Amongst the wolves I took my place along the moonlit lake and witnessed next a perfect gift for all my senses' sake. Dragons flew high up above and played a faultless tune- so golden were their lyres glowing brightly with the moon.

Dragons swooped and dipped the lake

> then up they went in shifts,

>> and played to crowds in balconies,

>>> that sat amongst the cliffs.

A Dragon sang into the lake and OH the flames did spew; the lake repeated fiery verse and flamed the word… **VIRTUE**

The crowd returned a hearty chant…into the night they roared. From high atop cliff balconies, their breathy fires soared! Once echoes left from final note and made the whole earth shake; fell from the cliffs a ball of fire that sizzled in the lake.

The lake began to froth and boil and from its endless deep, came the word…**APATHY** in flames that seemed to leap! One Dragon flew above the flames and hovered like a bee, addressed the crowd most movingly then pointed straight at me.

"Apathy is a somber song and we've a peaceful guest, who's heard his share of somber notes so somber we must best. A higher path he's chosen forth within this vital quest; so on our players will to play and play at HIS bequest!"

Before my feet the Dragon laid three stones of equal size, and said to choose whichever one most pleasing to my eyes. I placed my hand above the stones, all senses to perceive, then closed my eyes to choose the one as sometimes eyes deceive. From left to right I moved my hand till warmth became quite clear. I grabbed the stone and held it high…which brought a scorching cheer! The Dragon breathed onto the stone until a rosy glow, then plunged the stone into the lake that sparkled far below. A shooting splash of fiery plume spread out and far above; the titled words of chosen song…

46

SOON I TEACHER OF LOVE

And so they sang this song that night through dotted stars a million bright. Most brilliant song to fill my ears; drained all my doubts, dashed all my fears. The chorus spelled for all to see, through flaming lungs in balconies. No truer words were ever seen, as what was seen is following…

THE CHOICE TO LOVE IS YOURS ALONE,
A LIFE ALONE FORSAKES.
A LIFE HE CHOOSE BECAUSE OF FEAR,
ALONE A LIFE HE MAKES.

Amongst the wolves felt warm and tight, as Dragons played throughout the night. The lapping waves and soothing song soon made my eyes blink deep and long. And when I woke to morning chill, to view the lake of bluish still; the footprints told of wolves retreat and Dragon's lyre rest at my feet!

❖ ❖ ❖

Chapter VII

ONES VOICE FOR TO HEAL

I walked from the shores with the lake at my back, carrying the Dragons' magic lyre in my sack. Reliving the songs and night filled with fun, while plodding I did towards the bright rising sun. I picked up a trail with wind beginning to speak; below a deep valley of dotted lakes and snow peaks.

Stumbling over-then up- then straight down at a slant; through the rifts in the cliffs I must have looked like an ant. Then came before me and more than a mile, a twisting rock slide coiled down in a spiral! I took a deep breath, jumped in with a shout. Like a pretzel my stomach twisted inside and out!

There've been many slides that I've slid in my past,
but never like this one, this long and this fast!

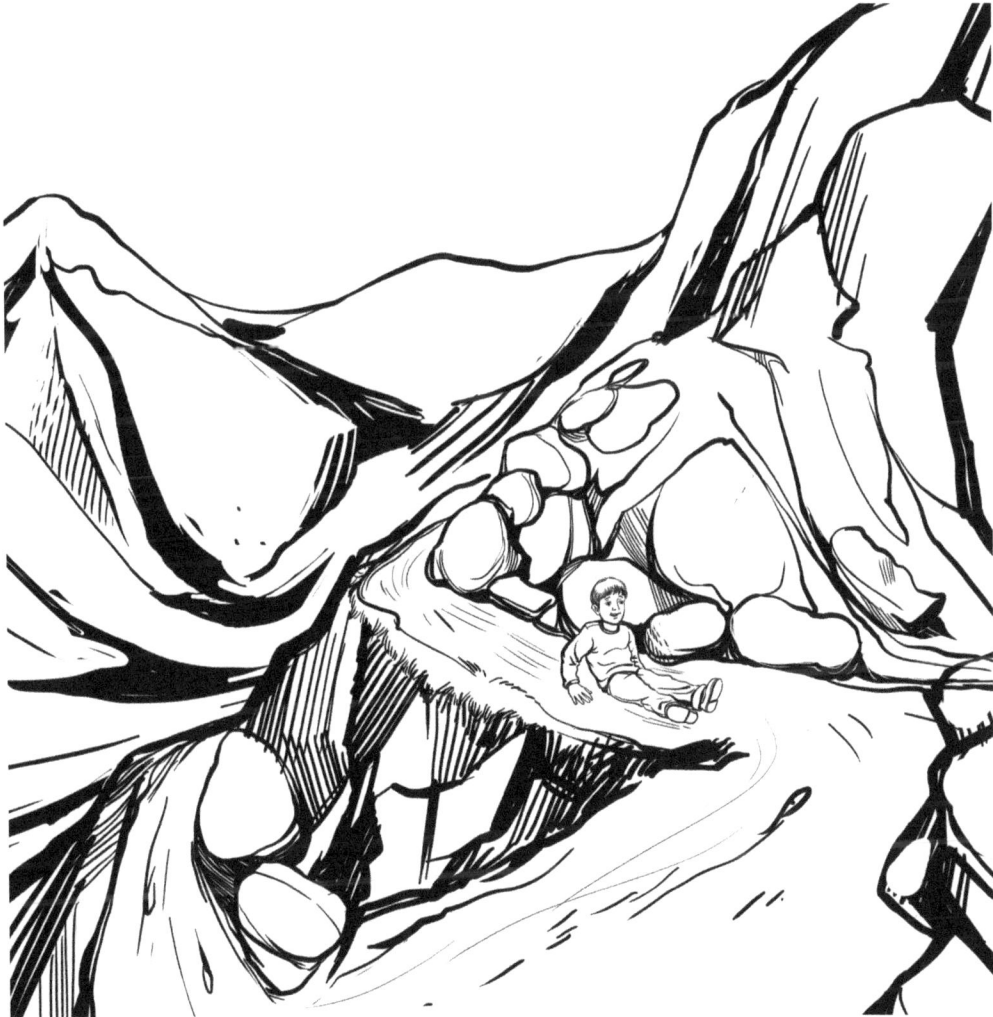

As smooth as a window that slide seemed to glide. No way could I slow as I tried and I tried. The slide it would circle…then shoot down in a swoop! It even one time twisted in a full loop! Abruptly I landed with feet over my head, in puffy soft moss that was thick as a bed.

I heard a sharp whistle and wind blew my hair. Then a lowly loud grumble and quick pull of air. Slowly I turned in astonishment to see…three sleeping GIANTS snoring loudly by me!

Shallow breaths I inhaled and slight moves I did make; for I really and truly don't want them awake! As I tip-toed unhurried not a giant to rouse, I slipped on a stone then heard screams... **"IT'S A MOUSE!"**

The giants jumped up bouncing high as a tree; landed quite hard then most vigorously, started heaving large boulders straight down and towards ME!

The boulders were crashing then bouncing instead;

Some of them bouncing right over my head!

I ran

and I jumped

and I dipped through the grind,

as boulders kept smashing and crashing behind! At path's end a stone wall; I reached high as I could- with nowhere to turn I was trapped where I stood! As boulders approached, the wall opened a hair;

I slipped through a crack with just SECONDS to spare!

Behind me the wall quickly closed the thin crack. The boulders they slammed with a mighty loud *THWACK!* Wiping sweat from my brow when hot breath I could feel; smiling down was a bear...his paws turning a wheel.

He kept spinning the wheel; the wall closed with a click. For as big as he was he sure spun around pretty quick and reached out his paw; I stretched high for a shake- His deafening laugh was a sound I would take.

"Thank you!" I said, with a breath and a pant.

He stared for a bit and spoke with a rant.

"What a story you have! What a time to relive! The pleasure is mine so no thanks must you give. You're surprised I can see, with a bear such as me, so introductions are due…I'm from Clan Bartlebee! Your journey's been long, you must be famished at least; so at once you must come to our gathering feast!"

We climbed over ridges to see valleys below of twisted shade trees above streams of blue flow. As we entered the trees of high soaring retreat I heard the low thump of many drums in full beat. The twisting of trees finally stole the sunlight, but the flicker of lanterns soon brought my sight right. And that what was seen from what lantern light brings, were several plump bears happily bathing in springs.

We walked past the bears, they hardly gave us a look, as they splashed and they laughed in their bubbling brook. We came to two arrows in tree branches lit bright.

To the left   **EMPATHY**   **RESENTMENT**   to right.

←   →

He normally led but waited on me now instead, as I pointed far left from the words that I'd read. He gleamed from this choice most curiously, then chuckled you see as I too did with glee.

The drumming drummed faster,

        so quicker our feet!

        Once walking,

        then hopping,

        now running to beat.

We ran into a dark tunnel, my eyes squinting from glow of a blazing bright door under words…   **LET IT GO!**

The bear thumped the door with a powerful kick; it creaked gently open after a clack and a click. The room from beyond slowly came into view of a bear jamboree fifty more than a few!

The room was a flutter

with bears in a clutter!

The dust and fur flying…along with their sputter!

Their clanking of cups and the singing of songs followed notes from their flutes and the banging of gongs. Some bears sitting on tables, some standing on chairs; two of the bears were even tumbling down stairs!

As we walked through the room, sitting down in a pit, were bears in half circle by a hearth warmly lit. They motioned me sit by the fire on a rug, where lay a huge feast and a small earthen jug. I ate and I ate till my belly soon juts,

from apples
and jelly
and berries
and nuts.

And that from the jug smelling just a bit funny, made my body feel strong and tasted like honey!

From the bears came a murmur and a shuffle afar as one bear proudly stood and held up a large jar. He shook the great jar over top of his head. From inside a rattle and whispers soon spread. Holding out his fat paw…what dropped from within? A smoothly blue stone… the bear widened his grin. He lift up the stone, slowly circled the room and held it close to the fire that snapped in full bloom. From the stone came a glow, in gold-lettered flow. Shining bright on the wall in words TEN feet tall!

SO IN HIS HANDS HE HOLDS THE HOPE
OF KINGDOMS AND THEIR RITES.
AND WITH HIS WORDS THE KINGDOM REIGNS
AND WITH HIS HEART UNITES.

The bears began chanting at that what was shown;

over and over

in low grumbled tone. The bear looked at me from his high lofty stand and for some unknown reason …I held out my hand!

He placed the stone in my hand with a baffling glare; I held it up close and gave it a rather hard stare. It looked smooth but felt rough, as I twirled it about, and stood up where I sat without one single doubt! I held high the blue stone then flipped it around; put it near to the fire…but turned it face down. The words began showing, the surprise I could feel. In gold glowing words was… **ONES VOICE FOR TO HEAL.**

The music, it stopped…all the voices soon squelch. I heard several high gasps and one untimely long belch. I looked around the hushed space with the stone still in my clutch when a bear broke the silence and spoke words that were such.

"It has been written for ages in our rune made of blue, that with hands he comes forward and with words that ring true. To deliver a promise kept deep in our past; a promise of hope for generations to last. So, for kingdom be our part in what we can do…He may ask that of us in what we he see through."

I raised up my hand…the rune flat in my palm, the bear understood nodding knowingly calm. Then drumming ERUPTED with powerful blows! The dancers, they danced on the tips of their toes. The fluting, it flowed with a euphoric soar! The bears, they all stood and pointed to a door.

I walked through this door as the drumming kept beat… when the ground from below became slick to my feet! The drumming it slowed the further I went, as I tripped and I slipped down that dimly descent. This tunnel squeezed narrow, the ceiling fell low. The floor started rising sharply up from below! Through the tunnel a glow from a brightly lit hole; I slipped out through a spout bouncing up with a roll!

Above me and haunting was a bridge made from stone- a slimy black rock that led to Queen's throne. I clawed up the bank, despite cold splitting rain… and inched through the gusts down her cobblestone lane.

❖ ❖ ❖

Chapter VIII

A RULER FROM HIS CHOICE

*T*he wind began howling its passionate dare, and taunted my name through the whistling air. My presence requested with large metal chains; a lowering drawbridge commanded the same. And then I stood before her hall of wicked evil hiss- The pounding from the stomping feet was sound I did not miss! The trumpets, they blew like a thousand alarms; from her throne the queen rose…outstretching her arms. The silence befell as she took to her stage; my eyes on the Creature enshrined in his cage!

"Well my if it isn't our strange little boy, returned from his journey and our little ploy. The knapsack he carries is full to its lid, so in it I trust he has brought what I bid?"

I turned the sack over pouring out in the light; the objects they fell from the left to the right. The Queen smacking her lips with a flurried delight as she fumbled her fingers to all in her sight.

"So I see you survived the Leopards' long sword- that dreadfully disciplined mongering horde!

And the Wicketts, how nice to give you their book. Did you perform to their liking you miserable shnook?

The Dragons…I'm puzzled; freely gave you this prize. You must have been pleasing, at least to THEIR eyes.

And Clan Bartlebee with their vulgarly smell; this rune means you fit in and fit in quite well!

But nevertheless you have done what I ask; this filthy creature is yours. My gift for your task!"

The cage went sliding with a swat of her shoe; inside his prison blinked the Creature I knew. The crowd began chanting in unified voice,

Louder and Louder…

"A RULER FROM HIS CHOICE!"

The queen raised her arms as if leading a band; spun around, faced me, made a fist with her hand.

"The time has now come to declare nation's voice! So tell me now little pet…WHAT IS YOUR CHOICE?"

The room became quiet from Queen's little fit; to defy her demands means I rot in the pit. To declare her the ruler brings chaos and fear; the evil draws closer- my decision looms near! And just as my hands began ringing with dread, a song started playing from the lyre instead! The same lovely song played from Dragons above; the same lovely song…

SOON I TEACHER OF LOVE.

The Queen started to speak but her body, it froze, as the book opened up to the Wicketts' wise prose. The same words that it wrote when last it appear; those words filled with wisdom…

CHOOSE TO LIVE NO FEAR.

For now as my heart is beginning to grow, the rune started shining in Bartlebee flow. The same words that glistened with golden appeal; in beautiful words was…

ONES VOICE FOR TO HEAL.

The question was that of which way was the right- and remained was this question, still enshrouding my sight. With fear still holding with all of its might- the Leopards' crystal began shining a brilliant white light!

Piercing the room over her throne like a seer; straight onto the words…

EVIL SOON AFOOT CHEER.

But unlike before,

       as for now it could be,

             the dark words REARRANGED

               for all who might see!

It was clear to me now from within it arose. Those words could be arranged, however I CHOSE! I could choose what I wanted; my pathway was here! I stood up to speak bravely and without any fear.

"I choose… **L**oyalty of the Leopard,

        Originality of the Hare,

        Virtue of the Dragon and

        Empathy of the Bear!"

My choice as you see was a choice very clear! As loud as I could, I screamed…

"I CHOOSE LOVE NOT FEAR!"

61

The Queen fell to her knees in ghostly cold shriek; I gave a slight smile…my eyes started to leak. But last time my tear was of frightened young boy; this time was different…my tears were from joy! Wiping drops from eyes but one got away; straight onto the Creature in cage where he lay.

The cage began RATTLING and JUMPING about, as Creature was growing and growing quite stout! He broke right through the cage like snapping a twig!

The Queen growing SMALLER as Creature grew BIG!

Soon all began bowing…each one in the hall… as Creature kept rising to FIFTY feet tall! The Creature, he snorted and glared down at the Queen. Straight into a mouse hole she ran with a scream!

He quickly bent down, slyly gave me a wink; placed me onto his back before I could blink. With a tiny step back, then a gigantic THRUST! We soared out the door; left the castle in dust!

We went *UP* and then *DOWN* then *LEFT* and then *RIGHT!*
From far down below this world came into sight.
I saw blue twisting streams of Clan Bartlebee;
Flew over those giants, still sleeping…all three!

Then swift through the mountains creating a wake, where Dragon cathedrals admired the lake.

Straight into the trees that lay waiting to snip; we whipped through them all with a powerful zip!

He dipped to the left to see Wicketts' sharp caves, of crackly thin fissures and crashing gray waves.

Brown clumps in the trees, as my eyes could just make, were Frowns fast asleep on their long summer break.

He skimmed the Leopards' ocean of emerald glass; then circled two times atop hillsides of grass.

We rolled swiftly over then shot up with a flair, to swim above clouds with my hands in the air!

Then slowly down in a spiral…without much surprise, met soft ground in the middle from earth on the rise.

The Creature lay down as I slid off his wing; when quiet reunion the stillness did bring. He sniffed at my hair as I hugged his warm nose, and gave me a bow from my head to his toes. Then up like a rocket he SHOT through the air! I followed his path through dampened long stare. He pierced through the clouds scripting high for my view; two words he did write and those words were… **THANK YOU!**

At once I soon noticed from shadowy ground a tree right behind as I spun quick around. The same tree that began this journey profound; that same tree deep within… my cape was soon found!

❖ ❖ ❖

Chapter VIV

"The lessons you learned on your journey alone
are yours for the taking to make for your own."

I looked back to this world for one final last take, put the hood on my head…the tree started to shake! Soon wind began pulling its whistling drawl; it felt rather like shooting straight up through a straw! And just like before as it was in the past, I thought I flew right through, three giant circles falling fast of...

Yellow,

Red,

And Blue.

And then I fell into a spin, a room came into view, of whirling walls and picture frames- then stopping on a cue!

I pulled back the hood barely over my brow to see for a spell where it was I was NOW! But then I recalled for I saw where I sat, that smiling old man in gray suit and green hat. He spoke quite relaxing and with a slight grin.

"It seems you enjoyed all the places you've been. I see by your smile and eyes I can tell, that given your choices you chose them quite well! The lessons you learned on your journey alone are yours for the taking to make for your own. And whenever comes doubt, in any affairs, always remember...

The Leopards, Hares, Dragons and Bears!"

He tussled my hair as we walked through the door; I skipped down the hall barely touching the floor. And back to the place with my steps I retrace when I saw what I saw was a familiar face! I ran at full speed and jumped high for a hug. In Mother's soft arms I felt warm and quite snug. She nodded behind me, then gave me a pat…the old man disappeared with a *TILT* of his hat! I looked back in wonder; a moment to peer, when Mother's sweet words made their way to my ear.

"I'm sorry for your day, as I wished for your eyes, was packed with adventure and full of surprise. But proud you have made me; my heart it has leapt, as your promise to me was UNDOUBTEDLY kept! And as you can see, the work day is now done. What remains is all ours…the night you have won!

So how will it be?" She said poking my chin. "The choice is all yours so where to begin?"

I know what she said before all this began. If promise I kept then the night was my plan. Whatever I wanted, with infinite play! I knew I could choose in what manner I may. But as soon as I pondered a night all for me I thought of the Creature that helped me to see, that love can be good to receive from the other, but greatest is love when you GIVE to another!

The adventure I had was enough for my day. My decision was easy once I saw it this way. I thought it quite fitting for my mother to choose…

After all, it was her feet that stood all day in her shoes!

"My choice is for you to get whatever YOU wish; perhaps some warm slippers and ice cream in a dish? The night is for you for however your path. For me, all I want…is grilled cheese and a bath."

She leaned down to kiss me, the rest was a ball, as we ran and we laughed arm and arm down the hall! Right out of the door and within the cool air, I dove into our car without even a care. The world was less scary; kinda like it was new… a little bit different at least to my view.

The sky was much higher!

The trees full array!

Porter Stone Manor, it beamed in majestically sway!

The road in slow rhythm like spelling a letter… at this very moment life couldn't be better!

I did sorely miss the kind Creature from there; the Creature that loved me and helped me to care. And just when I thought I'd never see him again, I rolled down the window to air rushing in; for up in the sky looked like Creature from far, which was shaped like a cloud and followed our car!

I giggled a moment for no more could be strife, as I knew he was with me…and would be for life!

I threw my arms in the air as wind picked up its speed, and yelled out…

"WHAT A DAY I HAD! YES, WHAT A DAY INDEED!!!"

❖ ❖ ❖

The End

www.ingramcontent.com/pod-product-compliance
Lightning Source LLC
Chambersburg PA
CBHW040247100426
42811CB00011B/1181